This Travel Book
Belongs To:

travel itinerary

DESTINATION:	DURATION OF STAY:
FLIGHT DEPARTURE:	HOTEL DETAILS:
FLIGHT ARRIVAL:	

	WHAT TO DO:	BUDGET:
DAY 1		
DAY 2	WHAT TO DO:	BUDGET:
DAY 3	WHAT TO DO:	BUDGET:
DAY 4	WHAT TO DO:	BUDGET:

DAY 5	WHAT TO DO:	BUDGET:
DAY 6	WHAT TO DO:	BUDGET:
DAY 7	WHAT TO DO:	BUDGET:
DAY 8	WHAT TO DO:	BUDGET:
DAY 9	WHAT TO DO:	BUDGET:
DAY 10	WHAT TO DO:	BUDGET:

NOTES:

Notes

Notes

Notes

Notes

travel itinerary

DESTINATION:

DURATION OF STAY:

FLIGHT DEPARTURE:

HOTEL DETAILS:

FLIGHT ARRIVAL:

	WHAT TO DO:	BUDGET:
DAY 1		
DAY 2	WHAT TO DO:	BUDGET:
DAY 3	WHAT TO DO:	BUDGET:
DAY 4	WHAT TO DO:	BUDGET:

DAY 5	WHAT TO DO:	BUDGET:
DAY 6	WHAT TO DO:	BUDGET:
DAY 7	WHAT TO DO:	BUDGET:
DAY 8	WHAT TO DO:	BUDGET:
DAY 9	WHAT TO DO:	BUDGET:
DAY 10	WHAT TO DO:	BUDGET:

NOTES:

Notes

Notes

Notes

Notes

travel itinerary

DESTINATION:	DURATION OF STAY:
FLIGHT DEPARTURE:	HOTEL DETAILS:
FLIGHT ARRIVAL:	

DAY 1	WHAT TO DO:	BUDGET:
DAY 2	WHAT TO DO:	BUDGET:
DAY 3	WHAT TO DO:	BUDGET:
DAY 4	WHAT TO DO:	BUDGET:

DAY 5	WHAT TO DO:	BUDGET:
DAY 6	WHAT TO DO:	BUDGET:
DAY 7	WHAT TO DO:	BUDGET:
DAY 8	WHAT TO DO:	BUDGET:
DAY 9	WHAT TO DO:	BUDGET:
DAY 10	WHAT TO DO:	BUDGET:

NOTES:

Notes

Notes

Notes

Notes

travel itinerary

DESTINATION:	DURATION OF STAY:
FLIGHT DEPARTURE:	HOTEL DETAILS:
FLIGHT ARRIVAL:	

	WHAT TO DO:	BUDGET:
DAY 1		
DAY 2	WHAT TO DO:	BUDGET:
DAY 3	WHAT TO DO:	BUDGET:
DAY 4	WHAT TO DO:	BUDGET:

DAY 5	WHAT TO DO:	BUDGET:
DAY 6	WHAT TO DO:	BUDGET:
DAY 7	WHAT TO DO:	BUDGET:
DAY 8	WHAT TO DO:	BUDGET:
DAY 9	WHAT TO DO:	BUDGET:
DAY 10	WHAT TO DO:	BUDGET:

NOTES:

Notes

Notes

Notes

Notes

travel itinerary

DESTINATION:	DURATION OF STAY:
FLIGHT DEPARTURE:	HOTEL DETAILS:
FLIGHT ARRIVAL:	

	WHAT TO DO:	BUDGET:
DAY 1		
DAY 2	WHAT TO DO:	BUDGET:
DAY 3	WHAT TO DO:	BUDGET:
DAY 4	WHAT TO DO:	BUDGET:

DAY 5	WHAT TO DO:	BUDGET:
DAY 6	WHAT TO DO:	BUDGET:
DAY 7	WHAT TO DO:	BUDGET:
DAY 8	WHAT TO DO:	BUDGET:
DAY 9	WHAT TO DO:	BUDGET:
DAY 10	WHAT TO DO:	BUDGET:

NOTES:

Notes

Notes

Notes

Notes

travel itinerary

DESTINATION:	DURATION OF STAY:

FLIGHT DEPARTURE:	HOTEL DETAILS:
FLIGHT ARRIVAL:	

	WHAT TO DO:	BUDGET:
DAY 1		

	WHAT TO DO:	BUDGET:
DAY 2		

	WHAT TO DO:	BUDGET:
DAY 3		

	WHAT TO DO:	BUDGET:
DAY 4		

DAY 5	WHAT TO DO:	BUDGET:
DAY 6	WHAT TO DO:	BUDGET:
DAY 7	WHAT TO DO:	BUDGET:
DAY 8	WHAT TO DO:	BUDGET:
DAY 9	WHAT TO DO:	BUDGET:
DAY 10	WHAT TO DO:	BUDGET:

NOTES:

Notes

Notes

Notes

Notes

travel itinerary

DESTINATION:	DURATION OF STAY:

FLIGHT DEPARTURE:	HOTEL DETAILS:

FLIGHT ARRIVAL:	

	WHAT TO DO:	BUDGET:
DAY 1		

	WHAT TO DO:	BUDGET:
DAY 2		

	WHAT TO DO:	BUDGET:
DAY 3		

	WHAT TO DO:	BUDGET:
DAY 4		

DAY 5	WHAT TO DO:	BUDGET:
DAY 6	WHAT TO DO:	BUDGET:
DAY 7	WHAT TO DO:	BUDGET:
DAY 8	WHAT TO DO:	BUDGET:
DAY 9	WHAT TO DO:	BUDGET:
DAY 10	WHAT TO DO:	BUDGET:

NOTES:

Notes

Notes

Notes

Notes

travel itinerary

DESTINATION:

DURATION OF STAY:

FLIGHT DEPARTURE:

HOTEL DETAILS:

FLIGHT ARRIVAL:

DAY 1	WHAT TO DO:	BUDGET:
DAY 2	WHAT TO DO:	BUDGET:
DAY 3	WHAT TO DO:	BUDGET:
DAY 4	WHAT TO DO:	BUDGET:

DAY 5	WHAT TO DO:	BUDGET:
DAY 6	WHAT TO DO:	BUDGET:
DAY 7	WHAT TO DO:	BUDGET:
DAY 8	WHAT TO DO:	BUDGET:
DAY 9	WHAT TO DO:	BUDGET:
DAY 10	WHAT TO DO:	BUDGET:

NOTES:

Notes

Notes

Notes

Notes

travel itinerary

DESTINATION:	DURATION OF STAY:
FLIGHT DEPARTURE:	HOTEL DETAILS:
FLIGHT ARRIVAL:	

	WHAT TO DO:	BUDGET:
DAY 1		
DAY 2	WHAT TO DO:	BUDGET:
DAY 3	WHAT TO DO:	BUDGET:
DAY 4	WHAT TO DO:	BUDGET:

	WHAT TO DO:	BUDGET:
DAY 5		

	WHAT TO DO:	BUDGET:
DAY 6		

	WHAT TO DO:	BUDGET:
DAY 7		

	WHAT TO DO:	BUDGET:
DAY 8		

	WHAT TO DO:	BUDGET:
DAY 9		

	WHAT TO DO:	BUDGET:
DAY 10		

NOTES:

Notes

Notes

Notes

Notes

travel itinerary

DESTINATION:	DURATION OF STAY:

FLIGHT DEPARTURE:	HOTEL DETAILS:

FLIGHT ARRIVAL:	

DAY 1	WHAT TO DO:	BUDGET:

DAY 2	WHAT TO DO:	BUDGET:

DAY 3	WHAT TO DO:	BUDGET:

DAY 4	WHAT TO DO:	BUDGET:

	WHAT TO DO:	BUDGET:
DAY 5		
DAY 6	WHAT TO DO:	BUDGET:
DAY 7	WHAT TO DO:	BUDGET:
DAY 8	WHAT TO DO:	BUDGET:
DAY 9	WHAT TO DO:	BUDGET:
DAY 10	WHAT TO DO:	BUDGET:

NOTES:

Notes

Notes

Notes

Notes

travel itinerary

DESTINATION:	DURATION OF STAY:

FLIGHT DEPARTURE:	HOTEL DETAILS:

FLIGHT ARRIVAL:	

	WHAT TO DO:	BUDGET:
DAY 1		

	WHAT TO DO:	BUDGET:
DAY 2		

	WHAT TO DO:	BUDGET:
DAY 3		

	WHAT TO DO:	BUDGET:
DAY 4		

DAY 5	WHAT TO DO:	BUDGET:
DAY 6	WHAT TO DO:	BUDGET:
DAY 7	WHAT TO DO:	BUDGET:
DAY 8	WHAT TO DO:	BUDGET:
DAY 9	WHAT TO DO:	BUDGET:
DAY 10	WHAT TO DO:	BUDGET:

NOTES:

Notes

Notes

Notes

Notes

travel itinerary

DESTINATION:	DURATION OF STAY:
FLIGHT DEPARTURE:	HOTEL DETAILS:
FLIGHT ARRIVAL:	

	WHAT TO DO:	BUDGET:
DAY 1		
DAY 2	WHAT TO DO:	BUDGET:
DAY 3	WHAT TO DO:	BUDGET:
DAY 4	WHAT TO DO:	BUDGET:

	WHAT TO DO:	BUDGET:
DAY 5		

	WHAT TO DO:	BUDGET:
DAY 6		

	WHAT TO DO:	BUDGET:
DAY 7		

	WHAT TO DO:	BUDGET:
DAY 8		

	WHAT TO DO:	BUDGET:
DAY 9		

	WHAT TO DO:	BUDGET:
DAY 10		

NOTES:

Notes

Notes

Notes

Notes

travel itinerary

DESTINATION:	DURATION OF STAY:

FLIGHT DEPARTURE:	HOTEL DETAILS:

FLIGHT ARRIVAL:	

	WHAT TO DO:	BUDGET:
DAY 1		

	WHAT TO DO:	BUDGET:
DAY 2		

	WHAT TO DO:	BUDGET:
DAY 3		

	WHAT TO DO:	BUDGET:
DAY 4		

DAY 5	WHAT TO DO:	BUDGET:
DAY 6	WHAT TO DO:	BUDGET:
DAY 7	WHAT TO DO:	BUDGET:
DAY 8	WHAT TO DO:	BUDGET:
DAY 9	WHAT TO DO:	BUDGET:
DAY 10	WHAT TO DO:	BUDGET:

NOTES:

Notes

Notes

Notes

Notes

travel itinerary

DESTINATION:	DURATION OF STAY:

FLIGHT DEPARTURE:	HOTEL DETAILS:

FLIGHT ARRIVAL:

	WHAT TO DO:	BUDGET:
DAY 1		

	WHAT TO DO:	BUDGET:
DAY 2		

	WHAT TO DO:	BUDGET:
DAY 3		

	WHAT TO DO:	BUDGET:
DAY 4		

DAY 5	WHAT TO DO:	BUDGET:
DAY 6	WHAT TO DO:	BUDGET:
DAY 7	WHAT TO DO:	BUDGET:
DAY 8	WHAT TO DO:	BUDGET:
DAY 9	WHAT TO DO:	BUDGET:
DAY 10	WHAT TO DO:	BUDGET:

NOTES:

Notes

Notes

Notes

Notes

travel itinerary

DESTINATION:	DURATION OF STAY:

FLIGHT DEPARTURE:	HOTEL DETAILS:

FLIGHT ARRIVAL:	

	WHAT TO DO:	BUDGET:
DAY 1		

	WHAT TO DO:	BUDGET:
DAY 2		

	WHAT TO DO:	BUDGET:
DAY 3		

	WHAT TO DO:	BUDGET:
DAY 4		

DAY 5	WHAT TO DO:	BUDGET:
DAY 6	WHAT TO DO:	BUDGET:
DAY 7	WHAT TO DO:	BUDGET:
DAY 8	WHAT TO DO:	BUDGET:
DAY 9	WHAT TO DO:	BUDGET:
DAY 10	WHAT TO DO:	BUDGET:

NOTES:

Notes

Notes

Notes

Notes

travel itinerary

DESTINATION:	DURATION OF STAY:
FLIGHT DEPARTURE:	HOTEL DETAILS:
FLIGHT ARRIVAL:	

	WHAT TO DO:	BUDGET:
DAY 1		
DAY 2	WHAT TO DO:	BUDGET:
DAY 3	WHAT TO DO:	BUDGET:
DAY 4	WHAT TO DO:	BUDGET:

	WHAT TO DO:	BUDGET:
DAY 5		

	WHAT TO DO:	BUDGET:
DAY 6		

	WHAT TO DO:	BUDGET:
DAY 7		

	WHAT TO DO:	BUDGET:
DAY 8		

	WHAT TO DO:	BUDGET:
DAY 9		

	WHAT TO DO:	BUDGET:
DAY 10		

NOTES:

Notes

Notes

Notes

Notes

travel itinerary

DESTINATION:	DURATION OF STAY:
FLIGHT DEPARTURE:	HOTEL DETAILS:
FLIGHT ARRIVAL:	

	WHAT TO DO:	BUDGET:
DAY 1		
DAY 2	WHAT TO DO:	BUDGET:
DAY 3	WHAT TO DO:	BUDGET:
DAY 4	WHAT TO DO:	BUDGET:

DAY 5	WHAT TO DO:	BUDGET:
DAY 6	WHAT TO DO:	BUDGET:
DAY 7	WHAT TO DO:	BUDGET:
DAY 8	WHAT TO DO:	BUDGET:
DAY 9	WHAT TO DO:	BUDGET:
DAY 10	WHAT TO DO:	BUDGET:

NOTES:

Notes

Notes

Notes

Notes

Made in the USA
Middletown, DE
02 August 2023

36147497R00057